Quotes for Personal Excellence – 3

Success

One Hundred Quotes and Thoughts
with One Hundred Insightful Illustrations of Lord Ganesha

R.N. Kogata • Lalita Kogata

DK PRINTWORLD
Publishers of Indian Traditions

First Published in India, 2014
ISBN 13: 978-81-246-0671-1
ISBN 10: 81-246-0671-4

A creation of:
Mr R.N. Kogata and Mrs Lalita Kogata
608, Hiran Magari, Sector - 11, Udaipur, India
Phones: +91-94141 58870, +91-294-258 3870
devkush@rediffmail.com

Printed and published by:
D.K. Printworld (P) Ltd.
'Vedasri', F-395, Sudarshan Park
(Metro Station: Ramesh Nagar), New Delhi - 110 015
Phones: 011-2545 3975 / 2546 6019   Fax: 011-2546 5926
e-mail: indology@dkprintworld.com   Web: www.dkprintworld.com

Preface

Success has different meanings for different people. For a politician it may be attainment of power; for an entrepreneur, amassing wealth; for an artist, achieving fame; for a family man, raising responsible kids; for an athlete, breaking previous records; for a scientist, the invention or discovery of something new and for yet another man, it may be the realization that all this is useless and he may feel fulfilled leading a simple life.

Everyone aspires for success. Success is attainable by all, irrespective of who we are, what we are or where we are. We cannot feel genuinely happy for a long, if we feel like a failure within.

Everyone should achieve success and you can realize it with ease provided you go about it the right way. There is no reason why you cannot conquer the heights of aspirations, if you know the rules and apply them in your life. You have to work yourself and no one can do it for you. Climbing the ladder of success is like climbing a mountain. Every peak is a destination, you climb one peak at a time but understand that the success is a journey, not the destination and you have to keep moving ahead. You have to climb your own steps, and there is always room at the top, you just have to know your way up.

Success depends on planning and its execution, and also on opportunity and talent, but not on luck. There are no short cuts to success; it requires hardwork and dedication. Luck may, at times, appear to play an important role, but luck is known to knock on the door of the deserving, others do not hear the knock. The one basic law that governs all success is that rewards in life are in direct proportion to our effort, and that we, and only we, can make it happen.

You should clear your mind of all negative thoughts and concentrate on solic achievement. Dream big but be practical and work to achieve it. Look at the successfu people around you. If others can do it, you can do it too. The difference between a lose and a winner is the difference in their willingness and readiness to change, improve anc achieve.

Set your targets, which help you to realize your goals more easily, and targets should be ir accordance with your inner desire and aspirations. Understand your limitations anc remember you are the only person who can turn your weaknesses into strengths. Be a ma of action; take first step if you want to be the leader. A good idea is wasted if not acte upon. Lack of courage will make you a failure. Taking risk is inevitable for success an taking risk is an opportunity you give yourself. It is better to attempt and fail than not to tr at all. Take failure as a challenge.

Always have high regard and self esteem for yourself. Your own choice should not ge affected by praise and acceptance of others. Understand that outside forces cannot satisf your inner needs. Also realize that nothing significant can be achieved withou commitment and discipline and see that you are not distracted by other temptations. Yo should know that your life is your own and no one else is accountable for it, and therefore you should understand your role in your life and work on it.

When you struggle for success and do not achieve it, you become frustrated and this leac you further away from your goal. But remember that success is never final and failure never fatal, and therefore, what is needed is to continue trying and remain courageou Always know that you are smarter, confident and have more potential than you thin

What you have to do is to assimilate these facts with determination, realize your full potential and let them do wonders for you.

Given the fact that achieving success is easy as well as difficult depending on the approach we follow as also to give some assistance to our readers to achieve success comfortably, we have conceived the idea of this book. Make this book your companion and let these thoughts be your inspiring pleasure grounds for a successful life.

This book comprises 100 carefully chosen quotations on Success, created, modified and mixed. Some of the thoughts presented are ours, others are from the people who have stood by and worked for the values, some were famous and others were ordinary people. We have acknowledged the persons who have been quoted, wherever we could remember. Our sincere thanks to all these great personalities and eminent writers who have given such invaluable thoughts to this world. Any amendment/addition is most welcome from the readers.

Ganesha gives peace, prosperity and wisdom and, therefore, each of the quotes in this book has a painting of Lord Ganesha to inspire you. These paintings have been created by our professional artists keeping in view the theme of every individual quote.

We prostrate before our parents Smt Kanchan Devi and Shri Bhairav Lal Kogata, and Smt Kamla Devi Nuwal and the late Prof. K.M. Nuwal for their benign blessings that have made us reach the present stage.

With the expectation of blessings and constructive feedback from all our readers,

Lalita & R.N. Kogata

Acknowledgement

Quotations from some eminent writers, philosophers and great personalities have been included in this book. Details of the same are given below. We sincerely thank all of them.

Page No.	Quotation by	Page No.	Quotation by	Page No.	Quotation by
7	Yolee Escuadra	40	Zig Ziglar	77	Maureen Dowd
8	John Burroughs	42	Mary Ann Radmacher	79	Jason Weber
9	Elmer G. Letterman	43	Thomas Edison	80	John D. Rockefeller
11	Helen Hayes	44	Vhonani Mukhasha Murovhi	81	Richard Brinsley Sheridan
12	Abraham Lincoln	48	Thomas Jefferson	82	Henry W. Longfellow
15	Helen Keller	50	Arthur Rubinstein	83	Benjamin Mays
18	Nisandeh Neta	51	Stephen A. Brennan	84	Eddie Robinson
19	Winston Churchill	52	Elbert Hubbard	85	Michael Irwin
20	Mahatma Gandhi	53	Mark Amend	86	Christopher Morley
23	Jose B. Cabajar	54	Tejasw	87	Denis Waitley
25	Bill Cosby	55	Josh Billings	88	Anna Pavlova
26	George Burns	58	Russell H. Conwell	89	Ralph Waldo Emerson
27	Amreen Ghoora	61	Joe Kapp	93	Thomas D. Willhite
28	Nora Roberts	64	Jim Rohn	94	Denis Waitley
31	Jane Austen	65	Evan Esar	95	Bob Dylan
32	Joseph Addison	66	Robert Collier	96	Raja Akhtar
34	Mark Amend	67	George Sheehan	100	Tom Hopkins
35	Anna Quindlen	69	El Dominiki	101	Jim Rohn
36	Bill Cosby	73	O. J. Simpson	103	Meryl Streep
37	Philippos	74	Vincent Lombardi	106	Winston Churchill
38	Chaz M. Harris	76	Robert J. Collier		

A ball has to hit
the ground hard,
if it is to bounce high!

A man can get
discouraged many times

– but he is not a failure
until he begins to blame
someone else and stops trying.

A man may fall many times,

but he won't be a failure
until he says that
someone pushed him.

A word of encouragement
at the time of failure is
precious than an hour of praise
on success.

Achievement is the knowledge
that you have studied
and worked hard
and done the best that is in you.

Success is being praised by others,
and that's nice too,
but not as important or satisfying.

Always aim for achievement
and forget about success.

Always bear in mind
that your own resolution to succeed
is more important
than anything else.

Be humble
in your success.

It makes your enemies
look weaker.

Become
a man of value
and not of success.

Character can't be developed
with ease and in quiet . . .

But only through
the experience of
trials and sufferings
the soul can
be strengthened,
ambition inspired,
and success achieved.

Confidence is the best buddy of success.

So always keep your buddy at hand.

Do not define your failure
by looking at
somebody's success

and

don't define your success
by looking at
somebody's failure.

Efficiency is
doing things right.

Effectiveness is
doing the right things.

Success is
doing the right things, right now.

Failure should
never go to the heart

and

success should
never go to the head.

Both make you fall in life.

First they ignore you,
then they laugh at you,
then they fight with you.

If you stay calm and firm
you would win.

For every person who climbs
the ladder of success,

there are a dozen others
waiting for the elevator.

For others,
your success counts and not your efforts.

For well-wishers,
efforts count more than the success.

And for you,
both your efforts and success count.

He who defeats himself today will become a great conqueror of tomorrow.

How do you spell SUCCESS?

Select your goal.
Unlock your personal potential.
Commit yourself to your plan.
Chart out your course.
Expect problems.
Stand firm on your commitment.
Surrender everything to God.

I don't know
the key to success.

But

The path to failure is
trying to please everyone.

It is better to be a failure
at something you love

than to be a success
at something you hate.

If you didn't succeed in something
– it was God's will.

If He made you fail in something
– then He surely has reserved something
bigger and much better for you.

Because only God knows what is the best for you.

So never be disheartened when you fail,
instead take the courage and struggle again,
because the best is awaiting for you at the end.

– Have faith in God.

If you don't go after what you want,
you will never have it.

If you don't ask,
the answer is always no.

If you don't step forward,
you're always in the same place.

If you have reached the top of the world today,
it is only because of the efforts put in earlier.

And if you are not yet there,
it is simply because
altitude of your success is even higher.

Just need to take a few steps more
for your dreams to come true.

If you live just for today,
make today the most successful,
happy day of your life;
I am sure that you will have an extraordinary life.

A successful life is nothing
more than a series of successful days.

If you want to be
successful in life,
be wise.

If you want to be
successful in love,
be foolish.

If you wish success in life –

make perseverance your bosom friend,
experience your wise counselor,
caution your elder brother,
and hope your guardian genius.

If you wish to gain
the success,

don't stare at the steps,
step on the stairs.

If your presence
isn't making any contribution,

why should your absence
make any difference?

If your success isn't on your own terms
and if it looks good to the world,
but doesn't feel good in your heart,
it isn't success at all.

In order to succeed,
your desire for success
should be greater than
your fear of failure.

Instead of getting pleasure
from everyone's failures
because you yourself are lazy,

get up and feel pleasure
from your own success.

Instead of having an **idol,** why don't you become **one?**

It is so simple to be successful:

Know what you are doing.
Love what you are doing.
Believe in what you are doing.

It is not what happens to you
that determines how far you will go in life;

it is how you handle what happens to you.

Judge your success
by what you had given up
to achieve it.

Live with intention.
Walk to the edge.
Listen hard.
Practise wellness.
Play with abandon. Laugh.
Choose with no regret.
Appreciate your friends.
Continue to learn.
Do what you love.
Live as if that is all there.

This is SUCCESS.

Many of life's failures are people
who didn't realize
how close they were to success,
when they gave up.

May your enemies
live a long life
to see your success!

Mirror reflects your physical being and not your identity.

So try to identify yourself.

My success is

having a roof over my head,
food on the table,
an amazing wife who is in love with me,
my kids that laugh and play
and don't starve a day,
and a job I love.

I don't need to be wealthy, but happy.

Never compare your love story with those in the movies, because those are written by scriptwriters.

Yours is written by God.

Nothing can stop a man
with the right mental attitude
from achieving his goal.

Nothing on earth
can help a man
with wrong mental attitude.

"Nowhere"
can become
"Now here"

It just depends on the way
you look at it . . .

Of course,
there is no formula for success,

except perhaps,
an unconditional acceptance of life
what it brings.

Our goals can only be reached
through the vehicle of a plan,
in which we must fervently believe,
and upon which we must vigorously act.

There is no other route to success.

Pray that
success will not come
any faster than
you are able to endure it.

Success doesn’t consist of
never making any blunders,

but in never making the same one
a second time.

Some people can't believe their own eyes
when they see an opportunity.

Other people turn
their visions of success
into reality.

because they

b

because they ar

Success doesn't depend on
making important decisions quick.

It depends on
your quick action
on important decisions.

Success in life is an addiction.
The more you are addicted, the more you achieve.
The more you achieve, the better you become.
The better you become, the happier you are.
The happier you are, the more likely you are to succeed.

Success is attained

by being active, awake, ahead of the crowd,

by aiming high, pushing ahead honesty, diligence, patience,

by climbing, digging, saving,

by forgetting the past, using the present, trusting the future,

by honouring God, having a purpose,

by achieving extra edge, serene thoughts,

by enriching life with broader experiences,

by cultivating determination to win, and

by striving till the end.

Success
is a combination
of your
thoughts,
words and
actions.

Success is like your own shadow.

If you try to catch it,
you will never succeed.

Ignore it and walk in your own way,
it will follow you.

Success is living up to your potential.
That's all.

Wake up with a smile
and go after life . . .

Live it, Enjoy it, Taste it,
Smell it, Feel it.

Success is never final
and
failure is never fatal.

It is courage that counts.

Success isn't something to wait for;

it is something to work for.

Success is nothing more than a few
simple disciplines, practised everyday;

while failure is simply a few errors
in judgement, repeated everyday.

It is the accumulative weight
of our disciplines
and our judgements
that leads us
to either fortune or failure.

Success is the good fortune that comes from

Aspiration,
Desperation,
Perspiration and
Inspiration.

Success is the sum
of small efforts,
repeated day in
and day out.

Success means
having the courage, the determination,
and the will to become the person
you believe you were meant to be.

Success without honour
is like food without salt . . .

It will satisfy your hunger
but it won't taste good.

Successful people aren't born that way.

They become successful
by establishing the habit of doing things
unsuccessful people don't like to do.

The successful people don't always like
these things themselves;
they just get on them and do them.

Successful people
do not plan the result,
they plan the beginning.

Right results
always follow
the right beginnings.

Ten Commandments of Success

1. Speak to people
2. Smile
3. Call people by name
4. Be friendly and helpful
5. Speak and act in consonance
6. Be genuinely interested in people
7. Be generous
8. Be considerate
9. Be thoughtful
10. Be willing

The best REVENGE is
your own SUCCESS!

The day you take
complete responsibility for yourself,

the day you stop
making any excuses,

that is the day
you step towards the top.

The difference between
a successful person and others
isn't the lack of strength,
nor the lack of knowledge,

rather the lack of will in the latter.

The elevator to success
is always out of order.

You will have to use the stairs . . .

One step at a time!

The great successful men
of the world
use their imagination . . .

They think ahead
and create their mental picture
in all it details,
filling in here,
adding a little there,
altering this a bit and that a bit,
but steadily building and building.

The minute you settle for less
than you actually deserve,

you get even less
than you have settled for.

The most glowing successes
are nothing

but the reflections
of an inner fire.

The only limits
you have are

the ones you set
for yourself.

The road to success lies
in two simple principles:

find
what interests you and that you can do well,

and put into it
your whole soul,
every bit of energy and ambition,
and natural ability you have.

Success will reach out to you!

The surest way not to fail
is to be determined to win.

The talent of success
is nothing more
than doing
what you can do well.

The tragedy in life
doesn't lie in
not reaching your goal.

The tragedy lies in
having no goal to reach.

The will to win,
the desire to succeed,
the urge to reach your full potential . . .

These are the keys
that will unlock the door
to personal excellence.

There is not one single recipe
for success,

but the most common ingredient is
constant improvement.

There is only one success –

to be able to spend your life
in your own way.

They do it, but differently . . . !

Defeated do what is tension relieving.

Winners do what is goal achieving.

To follow,
without halt,
just one aim:

This is
the secret of success.

To laugh often and much;

to win the respect of intelligent people
and the affection of children;

to earn the appreciation of the honest critics
and endure the betrayal of false friends;

to appreciate beauty,
to find the best in others;

to give one's self;

to leave the world a little better,
whether by a healthy child,
a garden patch
or a redeemed social condition;

to know even one life has breathed easier
because you have lived.

This is the meaning of success.

To reach a goal,

concentrate first on the path
you are taking toward your goal,
not in the goal itself.

Remember,
you can't cross
to the other side
of the river,
if you don't
swim or sail.

To succeed,

do the best you can,
where you are,
with what you have.

Too many people go through life
waiting for things to happen

instead of
making them happen!

Whatever you want, you can have it, provided:

- You can state specifically what it is.
- You want it so badly that it becomes a consuming desire in your life.
- You have faith in your ability to achieve it.
- You are persistent in your efforts.
- You are willing to pay the price for success, whatever that price may be.

What is Failure?

Failure should be your teacher,
not your undertaker.

Failure is delay, not defeat.

It is a temporary detour, not a dead end.

Failure is something you can avoid only
by saying nothing,
doing nothing
and being nothing.

What is success?

A man is a success
if he gets up in the morning
and goes to bed at night.

And in between
does what he really wants to do.

When you put a date on your dream,
it becomes a goal.

When you aim for the goal,
it becomes a challenge.

When you beat the challenge,
the reward is success.

The bottom line is –
To have success . . . you need a dream . . .

You and your rival
want the same thing.

The only thing that matters is
who works the hardest for it
and has faith in himself!

You are on the
road to success

when you realize that
failure is only a detour.

You are truly successful
when you can look

back in forgiveness,
forward in hope and
up with gratitude.

You yourself are
your greatest asset.

Put your time, effort and money
into
training, grooming and
encouraging your greatest asset.

You
can't
change
your
destination
overnight,

but you
can
change
your
direction
overnight.

You can't climb
the ladder of success

with your hands
in your pockets.

You don't have
to be famous.

You just have
to make your
father and mother
proud of you.

You never know
how far you can go

until you get there.

You want and you get – that's Luck.

You want and you wait – that's Time.

You want and you compromise – that's Life.

You want, you wait,
but you don't compromise –

That is Success.

You will never reach your destination,

if you stop and throw stones
at every dog that barks.